TOUR OF DUTY
on the USS Arizona
DECEMBER 7, 1940 - DECEMBER 7, 1941

Copyright © 2023 Buehl

All rights reserved.

HERBERT V. BUEHL

Copyright

Author copyrights the following document. All Rights Reserved. Reproduction of any part of this document, mechanical or electronically, beyond that permitted in Section 107 or 108 of the 1976 United States Copyright Act is unlawful without the expressed written permission of the copyright author and publisher. International copyright laws also apply.

ISBN: 978-1-948210-17-1

Tour of Duty on the USS Arizona

Published By: Alpha Academic Press
Published in the United States of America
First Edition – English
Cover Illustration by: Waldemar Góralski

Table of Contents

Copyright ii
Publishers Preface iv
Foreword v
CHAPTER 1 1
   Assignment to the USS Arizona 1

CHAPTER 2 2
   My Tour of Duty 2

CHAPTER 3 5
   Our Time at Sea 5

CHAPTER 4 6
   Time in Port 6

CHAPTER 5 9
   Saturday December 6, 1941 9

CHAPTER 6 11
   Tragedy at Pearl Harbor 11

CHAPTER 7 16
   The Week Ahead 16

Herbert in the News 20
Herbert Meets President and Mrs. Bush 21
Survivors of the USS Arizona 22
Remembering the Fallen Heros 23
A Letter to His Brother's Family 24
History of the USS Arizonia 25
Rest In Peace 26
B I O G R A P H Y 27

Publishers Preface

Many people have relatives that served our country in the armed services. Who doesn't enjoy allowing them to reminisce with stories whether uplifting or tragic. I was blessed to have grandparents, parents, uncles, and cousins that served in World War I, World War II, Korea, and Vietnam. They all returned home safely. Their branches of service were the Army, Army Air Corp, Airforce, Navy, and Marines.

It was always a pleasure at family gatherings to sit on the edge of our chairs and allow them to recant and compare everything from the battles, terrible food, sitting in a fox hole in the rain, swatting bugs from the tropical forests, parachuting behind enemy lines even going days without sleep. These were the men and women who defended our freedom, however, over the past several decades, patriotism in America is at an all time low of 38%. We need to remember those that sacrificed and gave their lives so we can enjoy the freedoms that we have today.

As the generations pass, many of these oral stories will fade and be lost forever. We at Alpha Academic Press are always inspired to capture these personal stories and put them in print for future generations to enjoy and capture for their family's genealogical archive. I would love to go back to the 1960's and capture all the stories I heard from our family veterans that have long since passed but in most cases, for me, they are fading fragments of my memory.

It is an honor and privilege to assist the family of Herbert V. Buehl to capture his writing in print and offer this book for future generations of the Buehl family.

Dan Stanley
Founder - Alpha Academic Press

Foreword

They were called the Greatest Generation. Born in the Roaring 20's and came of age in The Great Depression.

So, it was for Herbert V. Buehl; born on January 2nd, 1922, in Monroe, Wisconsin to George and Frida Buehl. He grew up on the family farm, and later moved to Janesville, Wisconsin with his family.

Times were tough during The Depression; but, with hard work and determination, the family thrived.

After graduating from high school, like so many young men, Herb joined the Navy. Jobs were still hard to come by as the world was still coming out of The Great Depression; and the Service was a good way to learn a trade.

After graduating from Great Lakes Navel Academy as an electrician, Herb was assigned to the USS Arizona. Where he served for one year, until December 7th, 1941.

He was one of the lucky few to survive. Out of a Ship's Company of 1550: 1177 were killed, nearly half of the total casualties of the attack, and 289 survived. As of this writing, there is 1 survivor left: 101 years old, living in California.

On December 16th, 1941, Herb was assigned to the USS Farragut, a Destroyer, where he served for the rest of the war.

After the war, Herb married, raised a family, and worked for Wisconsin Bell until his retirement.

He never spoke of his war experience until asked to by President Bush for the 50th anniversary of the Attack.

This is his story!

Jeffrey Buehl,
Nephew to Herb Buehl

Photo Credit: Paul Thompson Department of Defense

Photo Credit: U.S. Navy Military Archives

CHAPTER 1

Assignment to the USS Arizona

I was assigned to the USS Arizona out of the Great Lakes Naval Center outside of Chicago, Illinois. Our training had been cut short because of the Navy's need to bring all ships up to full complement. We had 120 men in the 91st Recruit Company at Great Lakes and, 'out of that number, most of us were assigned to the USS Arizona. Only the men who were going to schools for special training, or who were sick at the time of shipping out, didn't go with us.

It took us three days by a special troop train to get to Seattle, Washington. We arrived early (5:00 AM) on the fourth day and were taken from the train station to the ferry landing. We still looked like raw recruits, all lined up, waiting for the ferry to come. We took quite a ribbing from the "old salts" who were waiting with their girlfriends, and maybe some wives, to catch the ferry for Bremerton Shipyard.

CHAPTER 2

My Tour of Duty

After arriving aboard ship, they had us muster on the foss'cle (Forecastle deck) to be assigned to our divisions. I was originally assigned to the "A" Division ·which was the motor mechanics, but I went to the engineering office and asked if I could be an electrician striker. They could see no problem with that, so I was then assigned to the 'E' Division.

The 'E' Division comprised four sections: POWER, was the maintenance of all electric motors; LIGHTING, which was the maintenance of all lighting circuits; IC OR INTERCOMMUNICATIONS, the maintenance of all telephone circuits; and POWER DISTRIBUTION, the maintenance of the four generators, the two switchboards and the testing of all electrical circuits. I was assigned to the power distribution gang and worked in that area until about September of 1941.

I had requested a change of duty to the lighting gang so I could broaden my knowledge of electrical work, never realizing at the time that this change would make me a survivor instead of a name listed in the shrine room at the USS Arizona Memorial. My battle station was also changed from the forward power distribution room, which was located near the center of the ship five decks down, to the aft repair party, which was located outside the radio shack three decks down, next to the doorway leading down to the passageway between the #3 and #4 gun turrets.

The USS Arizona was in the shipyard at Bremerton, Washington being overhauled and generally cleaned up, repainted, etc. since most shipboard routines stop during that period of time, I was assigned to a Navy yard welder. Whenever he had to weld on the bulkhead, deck, etc., it was my job to stand fire watch with a CO_2 extinguisher and put out any fires that might be caused by his welding. At the time I didn't care much for the job, thinking this wasn't going to make a sailor out of me. I found out later, when we had to chip paint, fire watching was a "racket".

We did a lot of chipping and painting on the USS Arizona, but I found out that that's what made our ship one of the best in the Navy. It was hard for me to believe that, had it not been for the threat of war, the USS Arizona at 25 years old would have been de-commissioned.

All the crew thought a great deal about the ship and were very proud of the E's with hash marks on the stack and gun turrets. The hash mark was a sign of repeat performance.   Once a year we had to prove our proficiency, always trying for the E's or hash marks.

After we left Bremerton, Washington, we first stopped at San Diego, California, then headed for Hawaii. I didn't do much on that trip over because I had gotten the mumps and was confined to an isolation ward. I'll never forget that ordeal either. My neck had been hurting me quite a bit, so I reported to sick call right after breakfast. I guess, since I was a new recruit on board, they thought I was "gold bricking" and just passed it off as a, trick I was trying to pull on them. At any rate, a few days later, my neck began to swell and one of the first-class electrician mates told me to go to the sick bay and "don't come back, or else". That day, I told the pharmacist I could not go back to my division because they all said I had the mumps. Before it was all over, I had infected about 20 more men, so I wasn't thought of too highly.

When the doctor looked at me, he put me in the sick bay with the rest of the patients, still thinking I only had a sore throat. I told him I couldn't swallow the food. He said, the next meal, "We'll put you I still got the on a same soft diet food. So, I mentioned it to him, and he said, 'Eat only soft foods."

By now, my mumps were really bad and some of the other men were starting to get the mumps too. When the doctor saw me again, he finally decided I had the mumps, put me in a special ward and restricted me to my bed. All in all, my first trip at sea was laying down. I saw Pearl Harbor for the first time out of a port hole.

Because the USS Arizona was an older ship, everyone slept either in a hammock or on cots. Each one of us had an assigned space. My first sleeping space was a hammock. We had two hooks welded to the iron beams that supported the deck above. Putting up one end wasn't too bad -- you could just put the ring from your hammock webbing on the hook. But the other end had to be cinched up. This required a good pull and knot to keep the hammock from falling down on the men in the cots beneath. Usually, the fellows sleeping under you would make sure the knot was going to hold you up.

To keep the hammock from folding around you, we made spreaders out of "1 1/1 x 1 1/1 x 16" sticks with a notch in each end to put in the two outside ropes on the webbing of the hammocks. In rough seas the hammock wasn't too bad to sleep in. In a few months I did get a cot which made that job a lot easier. Out of the 60 men in the 'E' Division, the three of us who survived slept side by side on these cots.

Our daily routine started with reveille at 5:30 AM, breakfast at 6:30 AM, and the day's routine at 8:00 AM. For those who had the watch, they went according to their schedules. All of us had our jobs to do, depending on the division you were in. When I was in distribution, we had to watch the load on board and add generators as needed. The midnight watch took megohm readings (a test of the insulation resistance of the circuits) on all the circuits and each morning gave the sheets to the chiefs in charge. They, in turn, saw to it that any needed repairs were done by their men.

The one job I didn't like in the power distribution was cleaning and painting the voids around the oil tanks for the ship's supply of fuel. The space was about 18" wide. Before we would go down there, the space had to be well ventilated. The painting didn't help a whole lot either -- the fumes could make you very dizzy. It usually took us the better part of the day to clean and paint these voids. We had two of these in our area.

CHAPTER 3

Our Time at Sea

When we went to sea, which was two weeks at a time, a good share of. our time was spent at general quarters, practicing our routines. When they had target practice, it wasn't always necessary to be at general quarters, so we did get to watch that practice. The gunners on the USS Arizona were excellent. The anti-aircraft gunner got so good the Admiral had to ask them not to shoot at the sleeve that was being towed by a towplane but shoot behind it. They didn't want to stop the practice because the tow airplane would have to take time out to get a new sleeve when it was shot off. The turret gunners were the same. They would shoot at sleds being towed by a tug. It didn't take long, and they sank the sled and had to continue practice by shooting at a destroyer's wake.

I spent the last three months in the lighting gang. I liked this work because it gave me access to the whole ship and a chance to meet more of the men throughout the ship. One day, Captain Van Valkenburgh called for a lighting electrician to replace some burned out lights in his cabin. I was dispatched to do this work. When I got to his cabin, there were two Marines standing guard at his door. They stopped me and made me state my business in the area. When I had given them the information, one of them went into the captain's cabin to clear my presence there. When the Marine came out of the cabin, he gave me clearance to go in. I thought, "If it takes all of this to get past two Marines, what must the captain be like?". I was pleasantly surprised.

Captain Van Valkenburgh was the most accommodating person I had met of all the officers on board. He asked me if I had ever been in a captain's quarters before. When I said no, he gave me a tour through his whole cabin. When I had seen everything, he said to me, "What did I call you for?" I told him, "To replace lights, Sir." He said, "I like to have them all tested at times." That was the only time I got that close to him.

CHAPTER 4

Time in Port

In port, when we had the weekend duty, on my time off I liked to look the ship over. I had gotten to just about every area on the USS Arizona except the boiler rooms. As I remember, we had six of those, but I wanted to have one of the firemen show me that area for safety reasons.

Another area I was impressed with was the manual steering compartment. That required 16 men on 4 large ship's wheels to steer the ship. Rating didn't mean anything if .it would have been necessary to do his job. The strongest men on the ship would be selected to take turns with this job. Fortunately, we never had to use the manual steering.

Our meals were served in the same compartment we slept in, so that meant we always had to answer reveille and get our compartment cleared of cots and hammocks. There were storage bins along the outside bulkhead to stow our sleeping gear. The passageways contained our personal lockers which were about 1411 wide by 20" high and 1411 deep. We had all of our clothes and toilet articles in these lockers.

The mess cooks, who were the east senior men of each division, set up the tables and benches that were stored overhead in the compartment. While we were washing up for breakfast, the mess cooks got the food from the galley in pots and platters. The food was served family style. We used heavy white porcelain plates and cups. The utensils were stainless steel.

The food was always very good. The senior rated man at each table was responsible for the conduct of the men at his table. After the food had been passed once around, you could ask for seconds if there was some left. When the food was passed, no one could take anything from the platter or pot without your permission. If anyone did, the senior man at the table would make them put it back. Most dinner meals included dessert of some kind, too. The mess cooks had to do the dishes, too, but that was done in the galley as I remember it.

There were movies in port on the fantail of the ship. The electrician mate with the schooling in operating the projector showed the movies from a special projector booth mounted alongside the number 3 turret on the port side. The officers and chiefs had chairs to sit on, but the enlisted men had to stand on the deck. For a while, we used buckets to stand on so we could see better. But someone had to spoil that by using dirty oil buckets that stained the wooden decks. Anyone caught using a bucket was put on report after that.

It was either 1940 or 1941 that all capitol ships rated a band on board.

This was really a great addition. They usually gave concerts before the movies and, very often, a select few would play during the noon hour. All of the band members were ammunition handlers during general quarters.

When we were in port and didn't have the duty, the men liked looking through their photo albums. The men who had been in the longest, and had seen many places, usually had the best photos to show and stories to tell.

Most of the men I talked to had joined the Navy to see the world, learn a trade and some to make it a career. The men were above average.   We never had to worry about stealing or foul play. There just seemed to be a code of ethics that everyone lived by. Before the war started, I thought I would spend most of my career on the USS Arizona.

We could either wash our own clothes or take them to the laundry. Each division had a certain day and time they could be dropped off.   Anyone using the laundry bought a special knit laundry bag with their own tag on it. Most of us used the laundry for convenience. Trying to dry wet laundry wasn't easy if there wasn't a space out of the way to hang it.

All the men who could go on liberty could answer liberty call when it was sounded. Before we could leave the ship, the officer of the deck had us line up in two rows so he could inspect us. our uniforms had to be clean and pressed and our shoes polished. At this time the deck assistants would hand out our liberty cards. As we left the ship, we would first salute him and ask for permission to leave the ship. When he granted us permission, we then saluted the quarter-deck and went down the ladder to the launch that took us to the landing pier. There was a short walk to the main gate where we showed our liberty cards again before boarding the buses that took us in to Honolulu.

The engineering washroom was just off our compartment in the middle of the ship. It was here where we could wash clothes, shower, shave, etc. The 'head" was on the second deck forward in the bow of the ship.

CHAPTER 5

Saturday December 6, 1941

To start with Sunday morning of the attack on Pearl Harbor and the Island of Oahu may leave you with a lot of unanswered questions. With that in mind, let me tell you first a little about the weeks before the attack.

Our routine had been to leave port on Friday and spend the following week on maneuvers and target practice. I'd like to say we were good at what we did, being very well prepared to defend our nation at that time.

About a week before the attack, the USS Arizona was scheduled for a degaussing test. This is a demagnetizing process to make the ship's magnetic field neutral against magnetic mines and torpedoes. While we were doing this test, our destroyer escorts picked up a foreign submarine in the bay. It was our concern to make it surface so we could interrogate the crew, but we could not get permission from our officials in Washington to do so. No one there wanted to cause trouble with the Japanese government.

The next week we were in port. I might say at this time it was never the Navy's policy to have all the ships in port at the same time. Of our eight (8) battleships, four (4) were always out to sea with their battle group.

On the weekend of December 7, 1941, the USS Arizona had been fueled and readied for our port leave, when we got word that our departure had been rescheduled for Monday. That meant all the ships would be in Pearl Harbor except the aircraft carriers and their escorts.

All of us were happy about that, thinking the Navy was giving us a break so we could do our Christmas shopping. We also knew our relationship with Japan was getting worse, but never gave it a thought that they would be so bold as to attack Pearl Harbor without our knowing about it. The distance just seemed to be too great between Japan and Hawaii. I will say we all talked about the possibilities and knew something had to start soon.

Saturday was a liberty day for me and my two close friends, so we went ashore. We spent our time walking around Honolulu and finally stopped at a nice restaurant to have what became our last meal together. We had told the waitress to take her time with us since we were not in a big hurry. We topped the meal off with a giant strawberry shortcake. Now it was getting late and, since we always walked wherever we went, we decided to head back to the Navy buses. The last motor launch left the pier at 12 Midnight, and we didn't want to miss it.

The night was dark and still and, since this was the last launch, everyone wanted to get in it, even sailors from other ships. The coxswain agreed to take everyone, which meant we were really overloaded -- standing room only. The gunnels were eight inches from taking on water, so we had to stand very still so the launch would not capsize.

Everything seemed normal. We had no blackouts or special precautions in the harbor or on-board ship.

CHAPTER 6

Tragedy at Pearl Harbor

SUNDAY - December 7, 1941

Five-thirty came early Sunday morning. For those who wanted to sleep in, they usually found areas other than their normal bunking areas. Since I had a cot on the deck of our compartment where the meals were served, it was necessary for me to get up.

Our breakfast was served at 7:00 AM. The tables had all been restored and the deck cleared for the day's activities.

The Catholic men on board were getting ready to attend church services aboard the USS Nevada which was moored just astern of the USS Arizona. My close friend, Kenneth Keniston, and I were standing by our lockers talking about what we would do on liberty that day. Kenny was putting on his whites to go to Catholic church service aboard the USS Nevada.

The electrician's gang had just finished breakfast. While we were talking by our lockers, a chief petty officer came running from the fireroom blower intake room, which was just off the electrician's compartment, shouting, "The Japs are attacking. Close all battle ports and man your battle stations." For a moment we just stood there, stunned by what we had heard.

One of our first-class electrician mates suddenly said, "If it's true, close those ports and man your battle stations." I closed one port, then ran for my battle station. I might say this was all done in an orderly fashion. We had been well-trained and disciplined for all emergencies. No one said a word. We immediately started running for our battle stations.

I had just gotten to my aft-repair battle station, which was the aft repair party, when the first concussion knocked out our lights. We used sound powered phones for battle conditions, so I tried to raise someone in the engine room which was our control center. I tried calling my control station but could not get an answer, so I went to the doorway which had a ladder going down to the passageway between the No. 3 and No. 4 gun mounts and straddled the opening. I didn't want to leave the area without authority, so I waited in the dark. I straddled the opening of the doorway, waiting to see if the lights would come back on.

Suddenly, in one big 'swish' there was a terrific explosion. The force of the concussion blew me down the ladder to the deck below. I landed on my feet at the doorway to the passageway, not knowing if I was hurt or not. Since there was no light, I didn't know if I had gotten hurt or not, so I checked my body over to see if there were any broken bones or bleeding. Fortunately, I checked out okay, so I stepped through the doorway into the passageway between the two-gun mounts. In the passageway were six or seven more men and three officers. Since it was dark, we couldn't see one another to know who would be in charge.

The door to the base of the number three turret was dogged down for water tightness below the water line, so this had to be opened. The explosion that had blown me down to this area had also consumed most of the oxygen in the air and our breathing became very difficult. You absolutely cannot make your lungs work when there is no oxygen. For the first time some of the men got panicky. I knew our only chance was to open the water-tight door and hope there would be fresh air on the other side.

Some of the men began to panic and began hitting the door with their hands. I dropped down to my knees and pushed open the four (4) dogs that held the lower part of the water-tight door closed. Someone else got the upper four (4) dogs. Then the door opened, we had fresh air -- so we could breathe again. After everyone got into the base of the No. 3 gun mount, we closed the door to save the fresh air and to make the area watertight.

Now, for the first time, we found a battle lantern for light. Our first duty was to make an account of ourselves to find out who was the senior person in our group. We found out we had three (3) ensigns and four (4) enlisted men. As we stood there, trying to gather our senses, one of the officers said, "My feet are getting wet. We had better report our condition to the bridge." We held a short meeting as to what to do, because we had not been ordered to abandon ship. It was decided that one of the officers should report our condition to the bridge. This officer climbed up through the gun turret as the rest of us waited for him to return with his orders.

He reported that the USS Arizona had been set afire and was completely destroyed forward of our gun turret. He then gave the order to abandon ship.

We climbed the ladder up through the turret mount to the gun turret. The gun turret has an escape hatch out at the bottom of the counterbalance that is about two feet from the outside ladder. When I came out of the hatch, I had forgotten how far off the deck I would be. I did manage to swing to the ladder mounted on the side of the gun turret and climbed down to the deck.

Fortunately for us, the wind was blowing towards the bow of the ship. The smoke was very thick and black from the burning oil and could have made breathing very difficult if the wind had been in the other direction.

Once on the deck, we decided to remove a raft from the side of the gun turret and throw it in the water over the side for something to hold on to as we swam for shore at Ford Island. There was so much oil on the water we couldn't find it after jumping in the water.

By now I was getting tired and the oil on my skin didn't help any for that either. The oil was so thick on the water that it made it very hard to swim. The coating of oil on my skin made me tired, besides what I swallowed made me feel sick.

I knew I could never swim to Ford Island, which was about 300 to 400 feet away, so I swam to the quay (pronounced "key"). When I got to the quay, two sailors were standing on the bumper and reached over and grabbed my hands, pulling me up just far enough to reach the top of the bumper. They helped me get part-way up, then said, "You have to make it the rest of the way by yourself." If it hadn't been a matter of life and death I would have dropped back into the water. With all my strength I pulled myself up on top of the bumper. Just as I had gotten up on the bumper a launch came by. The coxswain said if we wanted to get in, we would have to jump because he wasn't stopping. So, I jumped, not giving much thought to broken limbs. Ordinarily, I would have dropped back into the water because I was so tired. But I knew my life depended on getting up on that bumper. With all the strength I could muster, I made the supreme effort and was able to pull and kick my way up to get on it.

The coxswain headed for the landing at Ford Island and said the Japanese planes were strafing the ships and the bay so he could not stop to pick up any more men in the water. When he said that, I threw overboard everything I could get my hands on, hoping the men left in the water would find something to help them keep afloat.

Once we got to the boat landing, which was the near end of Ford Island, we walked to a shelter located under one of the houses not too far from the boat landing. Here someone had gotten some mattresses for us to lay on. Before we had a chance to rest, they ordered us out, saying the women and children from Ford Island were going to use them.

I left that room and walked to the far end of the basement. Here there was an officer taking our name, rank, and serial number. When I was in boot camp at Great Lakes, our chief told us, "You can forget everything including your name, but never forget your serial number." I haven't forgotten that to this day.

It was now mid-afternoon on Sunday. I was still a mess from the oil and hadn't had a thing to eat. One of the officers was concerned about some of us because we had no shoes and only our shorts to wear. He decided we would go into some of the officers' houses on Ford Island and find some clothes. All we had on at the time were our skivvies.

The house I went into had men's clothes about the right length but quite a bit bigger around the waist. It was at least better than nothing. When we were dressed, we went back to the shelter and almost immediately were taken to one of the hangers on Ford Island.

Everyone was afraid the Japanese would be coming back with a landing party and take over the Hawaiian Islands. We didn't have any ammunition ready for our machine guns. We were taken to an airplane hangar on Ford Island to help make up 50 caliber machine gun belts. We were told that the planes off the Enterprise would be coming in to be armed. Everyone was told that the planes would be coming in with their lights on so that we would know they were our planes. But they still got shot at. So, I spent the rest of the afternoon and early evening making up machine gun belts for our planes.

By now, I was really beginning to feel sick. I still hadn't eaten and the oil on my body was making me feel ill too. I stayed in the hangar Sunday night. I found a corner to get some sleep, but my head was starting to ache so most of the night I was very uncomfortable.

CHAPTER 7

The Week Ahead

Yesterday, December 7, 1941—a date which will live in infamy— the United States of America was suddenly and deliberately attacked by the naval and air forces of the Empire of Japan......

......The attack yesterday on the Hawaiian Islands has caused severe damage to American naval and military forces. I regret to tell you that very many American lives have been lost. In addition, American ships have been reported torpedoed on the high seas between San Francisco and Honolulu.

President Franklin D. Roosevelt

MONDAY - December 8, 1941

On Monday morning they had Mess call at 7:00 AM but I decided I had to go to sick bay. When I got to sick bay, I met a pharmacist who had gone through boot camp with me at Great Lakes. He was assigned to the hospital on Ford Island after his pharmacy training. He took me under his wing and helped me out a great deal.

He was really a life saver for me. He saw how oily I was and helped me get showered and got the oil out of my hair. It sure felt good to get clean again.

By now my breathing had gotten bad, too. I could only take a half breath so that pharmacist had me breathe through a water pipe that had some medication in it. After breathing that medicine for 24 hours I was back to normal.

The clothes I had taken the day before from one of the houses happened to belong to one of the doctors here at the sick bay. One of the doctors was making his rounds of the patients to see how we were doing. When he got to me, he recognized his clothes hanging on my bed post and that upset him. He was so mad at me that he wanted to court martial me for stealing his clothes. He picked up his clothes and stalked out. I never did have a doctor check me over.

My pharmacist friend came to my aid again and said he would get me some clothes to wear from his friends, which he did.

TUESDAY - December 9, 1941

I still hadn't taken a shower or cleaned the oil out of my hair, so the pharmacist thought I had better get the job done. I didn't realize I was such a mess until I started to clean up. My hair was so full of oil I had to have one of the pharmacists help me wash it out.

By this time, my lungs were in bad shape, too. I could only take half a breath before it felt like a knife was being stuck in my back. The pharmacist gave me an Indian water pipe with some medicine in it to breath into my lungs. a great deal. That helped my breathing.

WEDNESDAY - December 10, 1941

I started to feel better, so I was sent over to the receiving barracks that had been set up in the recreation hall. I was interviewed again so I could be reassigned to duty. At this time, we were given a postcard to fill out so we could notify our families of our condition. I also sent a short note to the family of my best friend and conveyed my sympathy to them.

The Navy was also in need of silhouettes of the Japanese planes that had attacked Pearl Harbor. They asked for help from those of us who had made model airplanes. I was just being assigned to a group to start making models when my name was called out for assignment to the USS Farragut, DD348.

That evening, after Mess call, they sent all of us who were reassigned to ships to one of the ammunition ships to wait for our assigned ships to come back into port.

Since our stay was only temporary on this ship, we had to find a place on deck to sleep. We all took a life jacket that was stored overhead in the passageway to use for a pillow and went to sleep.

THURSDAY - December 11, 1941

About two o'clock in the morning, a boatswain mate came down the deck and gave us all a crack on our feet with a club (this by way of getting you up in a hurry) and told us to report to the ammunition hold. A destroyer was coming in to take on ammunition. Some of the men had been assigned to this destroyer, so they went aboard after the munitions were all aboard. The rest of us went back to our life jackets and slept until it was time for breakfast.

FRIDAY - December 12, 1941

It must have been close to 10 AM when the USS Farragut sent a whale boat over for me. since I had been an electrician's striker on board the USS Arizona and had made that my choice in my reassigning interview, I went aboard the USS Farragut as an electrician mate's striker too. I was immediately introduced to the chief electrician's mate. He wanted to know all about my experiences on board the USS Arizona.

I spent one year to about the day on board the USS Arizona. The ship was a great loss to the navy in both manpower and vessels. We can only wonder what part she would have played in the war. The USS Arizona Memorial will always be a reminder to all of us of the sacrifices that were made on December 7, 1941. May we remember the price that was paid for Peace.

I was assigned to the USS Farragut (DD348). It was the first new destroyer built after World War I. on this ship I was involved in many encounters with the Japanese forces throughout the Pacific Ocean.

With a concluding note, though the attack on Pearl Harbor lasted about two (2) hours, I never saw I Japanese plane or heard a shot fired, even though destruction was everywhere. I can still see the USS Arizona giving off the black smoke from the burning oil. It made my heart ache. If you visit the Memorial, as you look down on the ship you can still see ribbons of oil floating above the hulk on the water. This leakage will continue for many years to come. Some estimate another 30 to 40 years.

Of the forty (40) men in the electrician's gang, only three (3) of us survived. We were all in the aft part of the ship. One was the electrician of number 3 turret, the other of number 4 turret, and I was from the after-repair party.

I was in the 91 Recruit Company at Great Lakes Naval Training Station. There were 120 men from the Midwest that made up this company. out of that group all but about ten (10) men were assigned to the USS Arizona. To the best of my knowledge, only four (4) of us survived Pearl Harbor and the war.

POINT OF INTEREST: The bombardier, Kanai, credited with the amazing strike that exploded the USS Arizona, was shot down and killed at Wake Island on December 16, 1941.

Herbert in the News

Sailor recalls Pearl Harbor attack

The battleship USS Arizona belched smoke as it toppled over during the Japanese attack on Pearl Harbor during World War II. The ship sank with more than 80 percent of its 1,500-man crew.

By DARLA CARTER
The Courier-Journal

Herbert Buehl remembers the bombing of Pearl Harbor as if it were yesterday. He was aboard the battleship USS Arizona when the Japanese attacked at 7:49 a.m. on Dec. 7, 1941.

"It was like having a bad dream," Buehl, 77, said as he sat in his eastern Jefferson County condominium, talking about the attack on the eve of the bombing's 58th anniversary.

Buehl, a Wisconsin native who was part of the ship's electrician gang, recalled how his emotions ran high as he and his fellow crewmen ran to their battle stations and were later forced to abandon the burning ship, which later sank.

Buehl, who was 19 at the time, and a friend had been standing in a compartment of the ship, talking about their plans for the day, when a chief petty officer came running through screaming that the Japanese were attacking.

When Buehl reached his battle station in a lower compartment, the Arizona was rocked by an explosion that plunged it into darkness.

"I didn't know what I should really do because you're not supposed to leave your battle station until you're given permission," he said. "I tried to get (in contact with) the engine room, which is our command center, and they didn't answer."

Buehl moved to the door

Herbert Buehl of Jefferson County held a photo of himself from when he served on the USS Arizona. He escaped during the surprise attack, but he said, "I was just a snap of a finger away from not making it."

This is a piece of a flag that once flew over the USS Arizona.

and was knocked from his feet by another explosion that catapulted him down a ladder to the deck below.

"This explosion was so fierce that it just picked me up and pushed me down there," he said.

Worried that he might be hurt, Buehl began feeling for wounds and broken bones. Finding none, he stepped through a door into a compartment where there were about half a dozen other men.

Some of them had begun to scream in panic. They could not see each other because of the darkness, and the explosion was consuming all of the oxygen in the air, making it nearly impossible to breath.

Buehl got down on his hands and knees to open the lower part of a watertight door and someone else opened the upper half, letting in fresh air.

The men then got a battle lantern and began taking stock of who was there to determine who was highest in rank.

See SAILOR
Page 5, col. 1, this section

Sailor recalls narrow escape at Pearl Harbor

Continued from Page B 1

"By that time, the water was already coming in, our feet was getting wet ... not that we could see anything, but you could feel it," he said.

"An officer in the group went out to report on the men's condition and found that the ship was on fire and all but destroyed. He returned to tell Buehl and the other men, "We might as well abandon ship. There's nothing left."

In a remembrance that Buehl compiled, he wrote, "We climbed the ladder up through the turret mount to the gun turret. The gun turret has an escape hatch out the bottom of the counter balance that is about two feet from the outside ladder. When I came out of the hatch, I had forgotten how far off the deck I would be. I did get to the ladder before dropping to the deck."

The men removed a raft from the side of the gun turret and threw it in the water toward land: Ford Island. But there was so much oil on the water they couldn't find the raft, which was dark-colored.

They jumped into the water and oil coated their bodies.

Buehl was worried. By then he was getting tired, and "I knew I couldn't swim to the shore" — about 100 yards away, he said.

He did make it to a quay, and two sailors "took a hold of my arms and they pulled me up until I was up about waist high, and they said, 'You're going to have to get up the rest of the way yourself,'" he said. "Normally, I would have fallen back into the water because I was so tired, but boy, when it's a matter of life and death, you get energy that you just don't know where it comes from."

Soon afterward, a launch came by and a coxswain told Buehl and the other men, "If you want to get in, you're going to have to jump. I'm not stopping," because Japanese planes reportedly were strafing the ships and the bay.

Buehl, who never saw any of the planes, jumped in the launch and made it safely to shore, where he walked to a shelter beneath a nearby house. In the basement, some officers were sitting at a table, taking names and ID numbers from servicemen. Buehl gave his information and then spent the rest of the day making up machine gun belts for planes.

But the effects of the oil on his body and hours without food began to make him sick, so he ended up in the sick bay the next morning.

For several months afterward, Buehl said, he couldn't stand the smell of oil: "It was just like somebody had put a wire around my head or a tourniquet and just turned it."

But he was glad to be alive and soon returned to active duty, helping to take on the Japanese in many encounters in the Pacific.

Since those days, Buehl has returned to Pearl Harbor at least three times. Going back the first time was the worst.

"You just flash back to all the men that were your friends," he said.

Most of them are now dead, and "I was just a snap of a finger away from not making it."

Herbert Meets President and Mrs. Bush

Beloit man meets Bush in Hawaii

By Neal White
City Editor

As a surviving crew member of the USS Arizona, Beloit resident Herb Buehl felt he had to return to Hawaii for the 50th anniversary of the Japanese attack on Pearl Harbor.

"It brought back a lot of memories. One of the things we did was drop flowers down the well of the ship. I'm sure many people said prayers regarding their loved ones that were lost. I know I did," said Buehl.

Of the 1,500 Arizona crewmen, more than 1,100 were killed during the attack. The ship, still visible beneath the water, has been enshrined as a memorial to the men who were killed on Dec. 7, 1941.

"It's just kind of awesome to see the ship still there. You certainly can remember, in my case anyway, what kind of magnificent ship it was. Now for the past 50 years its been lying at the bottom of Pearl as a tomb," he added.

While attending the memorial anniversary service, Buehl was also greeted by President George Bush.

Beloiter Herb Buehl with President Bush in Hawaii.

"While we were at the Arizona Memorial Center, President and Mrs. Bush came by and visited with all of the survivors of the Arizona. They were very friendly people.

"They are very gracious people and were very gracious and encouraging to all of us there. They wanted to know where we were on the ship during the attack and if it bothered us to be (part of the memorial service)," said Buehl. "They had such uplifting talks, you couldn't help but to feel good that these men didn't die in vain."

During his eight days in Hawaii, Buehl participated in numerous events commemorating the Japanese attack that launched the United States into World War II.

"There were about 4,000 survivors of the attack and their families there, and everyone seemed to enjoy the festivities. They had something going on all the time, you couldn't even begin to take it all in."

Survivors of the USS Arizona

During the Pearl Harbor attack, 1,512 officers, sailors, and marines were assigned to the battleship USS Arizona. Only 335 survived. Many of these survivors were aboard the USS Arizona during the attack. Others were away on liberty, attending training, or assigned to special duty ashore. Since that tragic day all of these men have worn the mantle of "survivor" with grace and reluctance. Many feel fortunate to have survived but some are haunted by the loss of their friends and fellow shipmates. – *From the National Park Service, U.S. Department of the Interior, USS Arizona Memorial, Pearl Harbor, Hawaii*

Survivors of the December 7, 1941, Attack on the USS *Arizona*

United States Navy & Reserve (320)

Name	Rate	Name	Rate	Name	Rate	Name	Rate
		FOSTER, James Park Jr.	Sea1c	MALCOLM, Everett Allen	Ens	THOMPSON, Norman	Mach
		FOWLER, Ralph Edward	BM1c	MANCUSO, Joseph	Sea1c	TRANTHAM, Glenwood Orris	BM1c
AMACHER, Charles Andrew	Sea1	FOWLER, Robert Dale	Sea2c	MANN, Charles Clark	Lt	TRAVIOLI, Vernon Alva	Sea2c
ANDERSON, John Delmar	BM2c	FRAZIER, Glen	CGM	MARCUM, Harry Bedford	CEM	TUCKER, Edward Daniel	BM2c
		FRYE, Everett Ellsworth	Sea1c	MARKS, Edward Joseph	Cox	TURNER, Richard Newton Jr.	Sea1c
BAGBY, Walter Franklin	SF3c	FUQUA, Samuel Glenn	Lt Comdr	MASTERSON, Kleber Sandlin	Lt		
BALL, Masten "A"	F1c			MATTLAGE, Herbert	Ens	URBANIAK, Edmund Leo	Carp
BALLARD, Galen Owen	F1c	GALLAGHER, William Fred	CEM	McCARRON, John Harry	GM2c		
BARTH, DeWayne	BM1c	GARFIELD, Jerome Harold	Ens	McDONALD, Don Erwin	Sea1c	VAN WINKLE, Edward Laverne	F2c
BASS, Edward Forester	F2c	GASKINS, Walter James	Sea1c	McFALL, Charles William	GM1c	VELIA, Keith Lloyd	Sea2c
BAUMEISTER, William Nicolas	ACMM	GAUT, Harold Woodson	Sea1c	McKENNA, Kenneth Kermit	SM1c	VESSELS, James Allard	GM3c
BECKER, Harvey Herman	GM2c	GEISELMAN, Ellis Hugh	Comdr	MELVIN, Earle Thomas	CFC	VIDAL, Daniel	MAtt1c
BEMIS, Edwin Wallace	Sea1c	GENEST, Dayton Merrill	Sea1c	METCALF, John Howard	Sea2c	VLACH, Vincent James Jr.	Y1c
BENNETT, Earl Dean	GM3c	GIBSON, Claude Clenton	Sea1c	MIGLIACCIO, Thomas William	Sea1c	VON SPRECKELSEN, Charles Albert	Ptr2c
BERDOLLT, George Anthony	FC3c	GILBERT, Arthur Barnes	Sea1c	MILHORN, Harvey Hollis	GM3c		
BIRD, Leroy Alexander	CTC	GILLEM, Charles "M"	Sea1c	MILLER, Jim Dick	Ens	WAGNER, Robert Eugene	Sea1c
BIRDSELL, Estelle	MM1c	GILLENWATER, Charles Ervin	Sea1c	MILLIKIN, Donald Hugh	Sea2c	WAGNER, Rudolph Louis	CBM
BIRTWELL, Daniel Thomas Jr.	Lt Comdr	GILLESPIE, David William	Sea1c	MINI, James Haile	Lt(jg)	WALKER, James Edward	QM2c
BODEY, Edward Raymond	BM2c	GLENN, Richard Clyde	Ens	MODE, Stanley Robert	EM1c	WALSH, Homan Leavell	Ens (SC)
BOWEN, Andrew Jackson Jr.	CMM	GOLDSBERRY, William Joseph	Sea1c	MOMMER, Rolland Earl	BM2c	WARD, James Robert	Sea1c
BRADSHAW, Harry Frederick	Sea1c	GORDON, Donald Eugene	GM2c	MURDOCK, Thomas Daniel	CY	WARRINER, Kenneth T.	Sea2c
BRAYDIS, John	Sea1c	GOSHEN, William Eugene	Sea1c	MUSICK, Clay Henry	Sea1c	WARRINER, Russell Walter	Sea1c
BROWN, Gene R.	Sea1c	GRABOWSKY, Leon	Ens	MYLAN, Jack Clement	SM2c	WASHINGTON, Joseph Henry	MAtt1c
BROWNING, Robert James	Sea2c	GRAHAM, Donald Alexander	AMM1c			WATSON, Howard Lincoln	BM2c
BRUCE, John Franklin	GM3c	GRAY, James Victor	Sea1c	NELSON, Grady Lee Jr.	Sea2c	WEAVER, Richard Duncan	BM1c
BRUNER, Lauren Fay	FC3c	GREEN, Clay Douglas Jr.	Sea1c	NEWELL, Bobby Earl	Sea2c	WELCH, Frank Jr.	Ens
BRUNS, Martin Benjamin	Y2c	GREEN, James William	GM3c	NICHOLS, John Edward	RM1c	WELLER, Oree Cunningham	Sea2c
BUEHL, Herbert Vincent	F3c	GRIM, George Edwin	GM1c	NIEMARA, Stanley Joseph	Sea1c	WELLS, Harold Leroy	Sea1c
BURCHAM, Jimmie Charles	Sea1c	GUERIN, Charles William Jr.	Sea1c			WELTER, Eddie Charles	Sea1c
BURK, Leland Howard	GM3c	GUNA, Andrew	BM1c	O'BRIEN, Edward Francis Joseph	Sea1c	WENTZLAFF, Edward Louis	AOM2c
BUSH, William Jack	Ens			OLIPHANT, Harold Eugene	GM3c	WEST, Mark Austin	CMM
BYARD, Ralph Duncan	CCStd	HAERLING, Howard Gustave	BM1c	OLSEN, Vernon James	Sea1c	WESTBROOK, Clinton Howard	Sea1c
		HAERRY, Raymond John	Cox	OSBORNE, William Daniel Jr.	Sea1c	WHITE, Thomas Arthur	BM2c
CAMPBELL, Frank Monroe	Ens	HAMILTON, Elsworth Fonzo	ACMM	OSMOND, Robert Hugh	FC3c	WILLIAMS, John Francis	Gm3c
CAMPBELL, George Kilgore	CTC	HAMILTON, James Edward	Sea1c	OSTERBERG, Vernon Magnus	Ens	WILSON, Charles Leo	Sea1c
CARLSON, Ray Christian	Sea2c	HAND, Vernon		OTTERMAN, Clarence Wayne	GM2c	WILSON, Harold Green Jr.	F2c
CARSON, Carl Malvin	Sea1c	HARGIS, Paul Eugene	Y3c	OWEN, Paul Ralph	Sea1c	WISE, James Louis	Sea1c
CHANDLER, Edwin Ray	Sea1c	HARR, Oliver Virgil	MM1c				

In the Shrine Room at the USS Arizona Memorial, a large wall lists the names of the USS Arizona's dead. A smaller wall (top of page) contains the names of USS Arizona survivors who chose to rejoin their shipmates in their final resting place. Each of these men asked that their remains be placed back into the USS Arizona. To honor this final request, National Park Service divers ceremoniously transport the urns of survivors back to the ship. Resting their remains in the sunken wreck allows them to finally reunite with their brothers who died on December 7, 1941.

Remembering the Fallen Heros

REMEMBERING A FRIEND: Herbert Buehl, one of the few remaining Pearl Harbor survivors, pauses to gaze up at the name of his best friend, which is inscribed on a wall at the Arizona Memorial. Buehl and other survivors are here this week for tomorrow's 55th anniversary of the attack on Pearl Harbor.

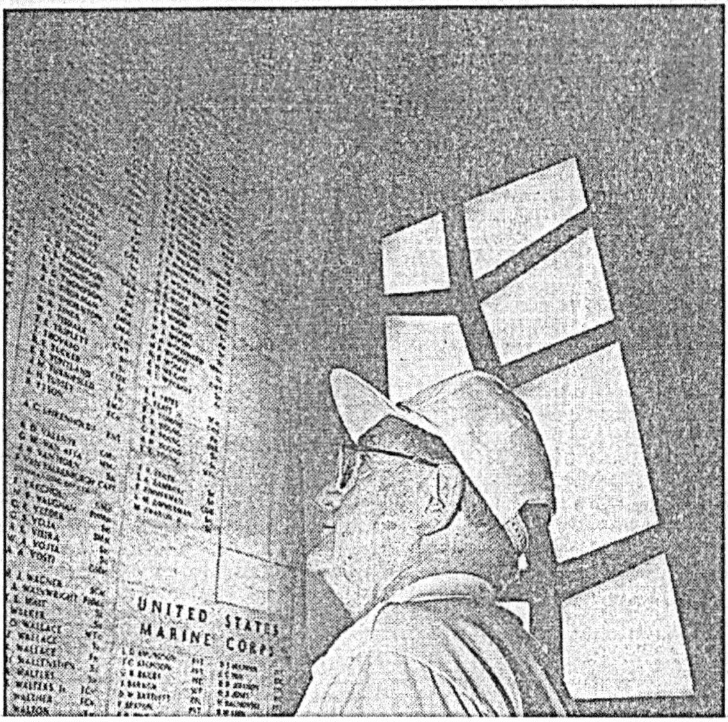

A Letter to His Brother's Family

Dec 13, 1999

Dear Willie, Donna and Jerry:

The article explains our Dec 7th day. Both Helen and Brenda gets together and made some calls to the newspaper and radio stations. They all interviews me and were happy to do it.

Many people gave us their newspaper, so we would have the article to send out to family and friends. Many members of our church were surprised to know I was at Pearl Harbor and on the Arizona.

The report for the newspaper did a fine job writting the article too. I hope you enjoy reading it.

Your Brother,
Herb & Helen

History of the USS Arizonia

- The USS Arizona was a mammoth among 20th-century warships, a Pennsylvania class battleship built at the New York Navy, Brooklyn shipyard and commissioned in October 1916.
- It was the largest ship in the navy's fleet, with a length of 608 feet and a displacement of 31,400 tons.
- It was one of the U.S. Navy's most heavily armed vessels with a (12) 14-inch guns, (22) 5-inch guns, (4) 3-inch anti-aircraft guns, (2) underwater torpedo tubes, each carrying (24) torpedoes.
- It was also one of the most heavily armored battleships in the US Navy. Its deck was reinforced with specially treated steel, and an anti-torpedo bulge was added to the ship's hull. Below the waterline, the USS Arizona was also upgraded with a double bottom — twice as much armor as standard warships. The massive battleship was designed to withstand a blast equaling up to 300 pounds of TNT without suffering significant damage.
- After shakedown off the east coast and in the Caribbean, she operated out of Norfolk, Virginia, until November 1919, when she made a brief cruise to France.
- In 1921, it was transferred to the Pacific Fleet, spending the majority of the next two decades working out of California.
- In 1940, the entire Pacific Fleet relocated to Hawaii, where it was based at Pearl Harbor in an effort to deter Japanese expansion.

Rest In Peace

BIOGRAPHY

Herbert V. Buehl, born January 20, 1922, in Monroe, Wisconsin.
    Enlisted in the U.S, Navy October 8, 1940.
    Recruit training at Great Lakes, Illinois. Serve aboard the following ships:

U.S.S. ARIZONA BB39, 12/8/1940-12/7/41
    Received the Asiatic-Pacific Area Service Medal. Survivor
    1 Star/Pearl Harbor 12/7/41

U.S.S. FARRAGUT DD348, 12/15/41-5/21/43
    1 Star/Coral Sea 5/4/42-5/8/42
    1 Star/Guadalcanal-Tulagi Landings (including first salvo) 8/7/42-8/9/42
    1 Star/Eastern Solomons (Steward Island) 8/23/42-8/25/42
    1 Star/Aleutians Operation, Komandorski Island, 3/26/43 1
    Star/Submarine Assessment, Pacific, 5/12/43

U.S.S. SC 1295, Sub Chaser, 8/12/43-6/44
    Operated in the Miami, Florida and Gulf of Mexico Area Put ship in commission.

U.S.S. ATA 201, Auxiliary Tug Attack, 9/11/44-10/1/46
    Operated in Central Pacific Ocean as far as the Philippine Islands, Okinawa and Japan
    Covered landings at Wakayama, Japan, October 9, 1945
    Put ship in commission.
    Left ATA 201 at New Orleans, Louisiana for Great Lakes, Illinois and was given leave October 6, 1946, until November 6, 1946 at which time my discharge took effect.

MARRIED Helen Voss September 3, 1949. Have four children.
    Worked for Wisconsin Bell for thirty-eight (38) years and four (4) months.
    Retired November 30, 1985,
    Lived in Beloit, Wisconsin